Herbs For All Creatures

by Ruth Jeanne Burton

The fruit will be for food and the leaves for medicine.
Ezekiel 47:12

Praise the Lord. The Lord heard me and healed me.
Psalm 30

And God said, "Let the earth bring forth every kind of animal - cattle and reptiles and wildlife of every kind." And so it was. God made all sorts of wild animals and cattle and reptiles. And God was pleased with what he had done. Then God said, "Let us make a man - someone like ourselves, to be master of all life upon the earth and in the skies and in the seas." So God made man like his Maker. Like God did God make man. Man and maid did He make them. And God blessed them and told them, "Multiply and fill the earth and subdue it; you are masters of the fish and birds and all the animals. And look! I have given you the seed-bearing plants throughout the earth, and all the fruit trees for your food. And I've given all the grass and plants to the animals and birds for their food."
Genesis 1:24-30

Out of the ground the Lord formed every beast of the field and every bird of the air.
Genesis 2:19

Psalm 104

COPYRIGHT 1991-2008
by Ruth Jeanne Burton

All Rights Reserved
Revision 5.0

Ruth Jeanne Burton
Apt. 5 125-S Club House Drive, S.W.
Leesburg, Virginia 20175-4221
(703) 779-2633

Available in Spanish

Ruth Burton is a manager with Nature's Sunshine Products and ships orders nationally and internationally. All of Ruth's remedies in this book are Nature's Sunshine Products and can be obtained from Ruth. A price list and catalog are available from the address above.

Ruth is available for free lectures. She has found from personal experience that most herbs work the same for people and animals.

PLEASE SEND ME YOUR SUCCESS STORIES TO SHARE WITH OTHERS.

TABLE OF CONTENTS

How to Order This Book	2
Dedication, Acknowledgements, Notice	4
Edna	5
Hugs	7
Introduction	8
Food, Treats, Toys, Tips	9
Recipes	12
Rescue Remedy	14
Identifying Snakes	15
Help Save Us	16
The Flood	17
True Testimonials (Alphabetical)	18
Garlic	55, 71
Alone Again	56
Kinship of Love	57
Dog	58
Pets Age Chart	59
Chlorophyll	60
Extracts	61
Capsules and Extract Amounts	61
Suggestions to Help	62
Organizations	64
Pet Eye Chart	66
Books and Articles	67, 68
References	68
A Prayer for Animals	69
The Donkey's Cross	69
The Horse's Prayer	70
Four Feet in Heaven	72
Little Black Dog	74
Pet's Bill of Rights	75
A Dog's Prayer	76
About the Author	80

"The greatness of a nation can be judged by the way its animals are treated"
    Gandhi

DEDICATION

I dedicate my book to my cat Edna who has made me learn so much because I don't want her to die.

ACKNOWLEDGEMENTS

Cover Art: Thanks to Evelyn Caissie.

I would like to thank my son Steve Sawtelle, my daughter Cherie Lower, and their families for all their help and encouragement.

Many thanks to all the people who have shared with me. God bless each one of them.

Many thanks to the authors of poems I have used. I could not contact all of them and they have added much.

I would like to thank Steve Sawtelle, my son, for the many hours he spends correcting and helping me add to each revision. I couldn't do it without him.

NOTICE

These are testimonies from my friends and me. I do not prescribe or diagnose. This information is to be used for educational purposes only.

Information presented about herbs and their effects is based on historical use.

EDNA

I'm searching for food and my mother. She would never desert me unless a car hit her. I'm a beautiful gray calico kitty with big lovable eyes. Oh, I'd like a drink of water or my mom's milk. Nothing.

A lady is picking me up. She cuddles me. I'm purring wildly with happiness. She takes me home in her golf cart.

I grow up but I'm much weaker than most kitties. My neck heals from being bit on the street; she put some aloe vera gel with VS-C on the wound. My body tries to die many times. Once I went to the vet for oxygen and intravenous feeding or I would have died. He said my kidneys and eyes were in bad shape.

The lady realizes I need a lot of VS-C; she muscle tests me for it. They call it surrogate muscle testing. She gives me bee pollen in my food each day for strength and longevity. She tempts me with mackerel (for people) that comes in a large can for just 99 cents. She puts herbs in it. You know God made all of us with a sense of herbs but people lose it.

I am now nine years old and stronger and a little heavier. Ruth has increased my protein. I get tofu, ground turkey, fish, and Energ V.

Chlorophyll in my water really makes me strong, and when I'm a little weak I get it in my mouth directly. It balances my electrolytes. It's organic alfalfa and has just about every vitamin in it. She doesn't allow me to eat grass which may have been sprayed with insecticides or herbicides. Cell salts would also balance my electrolytes.

She even checks my eyes for changes. She calls it Iridology. She said her eyes looked brown 12 years ago, but she has now had to change her driver's license to read blue eyes. She has learned an awful lot from the schools she has gone to.

We love each other so terribly much. Whenever she passes by me in the kitchen I jump down from the refrigerator or cabinets and land on her shoulder. I love to ride around on her. She keeps my nails trimmed so I don't scratch her. She gives me VAL extract, homeopathic Calming, or Rescue Remedy before she does this. It sure calms me down. I sort of run the gang here. I boss the dogs and other cats and parrots. Even the great big guys don't stand a chance against me.

We love and comfort each other all the time. Some time when you're born really weak you need a lot more attention. Ruth says when she's sad and lonesome our hugging each other always comforts her. They say it lowers your blood pressure. I know it sure feels good. Sometime when I feel bad she'll massage my paws; she calls it Reflexology. Or she'll hold me while she gently rocks on the trampoline to work my lymphatics. She also has Homeopathic remedies for lymphatics and pain. She uses a lot of these now.

She once gave me a Castor Oil pack on my stomach. It was so soothing and did I ever feel better afterwards.

I sure get a lot of attention. I think she wants me to live forever. She dedicated this book to me. I love her. I nudge her face when she holds me.

Thanks and Love,

"P.S. I take herbs daily, including E-Tea, an herb traditionally used by Native Americans. I also get one-half crushed tablet of ANTIOXIDANTS W/ PYCNOGENOLS (covered in butter) each day (I prefer the CHILDREN'S HERBASAURS). I'm older but stronger now as I once again ride on her shoulders and I play more. I am 15 years old now. She now gives me UNA DE GATO (CAT'S CLAW, IT'S THE CAT'S MEOW!)." Herbal Trace Minerals NOURISHES MY GLANDS!

HUGS

It's wonderous what a hug can do
A hug can cheer you when you're blue
A hug can say "I love you"
Or "Gee, I hate to see you go."
A hug is "Welcome back again."
And "Great to see you! Where've you been?"
A hug can soothe a small child's pain
and bring a rainbow after rain.
The hug! There's no doubt about it --
We scarcely could survive without it!
A hug delights and warms and charms,
It must be why God gave us arms.
Hugs are great for fathers and mothers.
Sweet for sisters, swell for brothers.
And chances are your favorite aunts
Love them more than potted plants.
Kittens crave them. Puppies love them.
Heads of state are not above them.
A hug can break the language barrier,
And make your travels so much merrier.
No need to fret about your store of 'em
The more you give the more there's more of 'em
So stretch those arms without delay

AND GIVE SOMEONE A HUG TODAY!!!

Dean Walley

INTRODUCTION

I was dying of many diseases about 22 years ago. I prayed to the Lord to get well. Thankfully I'm in good health now and look and feel years younger. I've been studying with many fine folks over the past twenty years now and have been using NATURE'S SUNSHINE products.

I've learned about many natural, wonderful, ways to regain my good health by attending many. many classes given by managers and different speakers. I've always helped animals but now I really have the knowledge to do so much more. I find that the herbs and natural methods I learned about for people work on pets too. How exciting and rewarding this has been. I was fifty three before I started learning these things but my children and grandchildren are learning early.

Many people like myself love our pets, but are on limited incomes and social security. We've found alternative methods to care for our pets and keep them very strong to avoid illnesses. We also like to help homeless animals recuperate and find new homes. Some groomers help and groom these animals free of charge. If each groomer helped a little, many more pets would find homes. Some veterinarians do some free neutering and spaying and try to find homes for the homeless. If each vet contributed it would really reduce the problem. Encourage your vet to help. A few vets allow homeless ones to to stay at their office for a week to find homes, but you must check to be sure people don't sell the animals to laboratories or just breed them.

HERBS HAVE BEEN AROUND SINCE THE BEGINNING OF THE WORLD. WE DON'T NEED TO EXPERIMENT ON ANIMALS IN LABORATORIES, AS WE ALREADY HAVE SUCCESSFUL REMEDIES AND THEY ARE VERY INEXPENSIVE. ALSO THEY ARE 100% NATURAL .

In this book I would like to share the experiences of myself and others in helping our pets get and stay healthy.

FOODS, TREATS, TOYS, TIPS

A well known holistic veterinarian, Dr. Joanne Stefanatos, in Las Vegas, is very concerned about the new type of kitty litter. You may scoop your cats' waste away, but you leave some germs and bacteria behind. She says that cats are getting serious illnesses from the contaminated sand. She prefers to change the sand on a regular basis.

My pets and I live as naturally as possible. It's really cheaper. We eat food as close to the way it comes from the earth and as unprocessed as possible. I buy organic vegetables and fruits when possible. We don't want chemical sprays. We drink Nature's Spring reverse osmosis water with chlorophyll in it. My pets used to eat grass but most of it is chemically sprayed. Liquid chlorophyl added to the water supplies oxygen to all my cells, builds strong blood, and deodorizes my body.

Our food is without preservatives such as BHA, BHT, ethoxoquin, artificial colorings and flavorings. My pets don't prefer a certain color in their food. I read the ingredients on food labels before I buy. I've found that the label 'natural' doesn't always mean pure. I muscle test items I'm not sure of. My pets get dry food with a topping of raw, inexpensive ground turkey, tofu, water, and lots of garlic, onion, and other vegetables. Many authorities use raw organic meat; definitely no canned products. I add herbs daily to our food. Extracts are the easiest to add. Historically garlic has been used as a powerful antibotic and parasite chaser. I use combinations when possible. Adding some food enzymes to our food would be very beneficial also. Absolutely necessary. There are no enzymes in cooked, dry, or canned food.

For treats, I give us nuts, carrots, fruits, white cheese, and organic eggs. My cats love catnip rolled up in a cloth. Historically catnip is good for nerves, intestines, gas, cramps, digestion, and as a tonic to balance the body. Also bee pollen historically is used to slow aging, supply energy, detoxify, and build health. I use ENERG-V. Adding a lot of garlic is getting big results.

For skin– Pau D'Arco or All Cell Detox—raw food—garlic—check thyroid.

We only drink diluted tofu moo. There is no milk in our refrigerator. Whenever I'm juicing organic carrots or other vegetables I add a little to their food. Almond is good.

I think vegetables and fruits are important. That is what Adam and Eve lived on in the Garden of Eden. They lived over 900 years. Daniel also grew strongest under King Nebuchadnezzar eating only sop which is a vegetable stew.

I use homeopathic remedies. They are so easy to take, but the herb combinations are the most important.

Cats love to play with a ping pong ball in an empty bathtub.

There are many organizations to help keep health costs down, such as low cost neuter and spay fees. Check with the local animal shelter.

When Edna refuses her herbs in food, I wrap her up in a towel, combine all the extracts into one dropper tipped with honey, and squirt it into her mouth.

Most holistic vets are giving vaccinations only when animals are young, not after that. Of course rabies vaccinations are required. (reference 3).

Please do not let your pets drink from the toilet!

The Heimlich maneuver can be used to aid a pet that is choking.

Animals don't get enzymes in cooked or canned foods. I use raw food and add enzymes too. Most holistic vets are prescribing raw meat and chopped raw vegetables with a small amount of dry food, brown rice, etc.

Don't put herbs in the pet's water bowl. You never know how long it will take for them to drink it. A large dropper or turkey baster with a small amount of honey can make it easier and pleasanter to take.

Noah's Ark

God would punish his wicked people with a storm
Frightened, they had never seen anything of this form
Noah, He said, you shall survive because of your strength
Gather together the creatures before the earth is rent

Noah was told to build the Ark
Whilst the rains poured from the dark
They would be safe from all harm
Noah paired them together in great alarm

Elephants, tigers, giraffes, and geese
They tossed and turned and waited for peace
Now forty days the rain came straight
Aboard the Ark not a moment too late

Noah and the animals waited for the sun
The rain had ceased, the end had come
All was calm and bright, brought by the dove
Noah had done his work for the Lord above

Amateurs built the Ark, Professionals built the Titanic

RECIPES

How can cheap dry dog or cat food be nutricious? It costs almost as little as kitty litter! What we eat determines the state of our health.

Ruth's Healthy Treat for Dogs, Cats, and Birds

1 pound partially frozen ground turkey or 1/2 pound tofu and 1/2 pound turkey
1/4 cup brewer's yeast
1/4 cup wheat germ
plenty of garlic
2 fresh farm eggs

Catnip can be added for kitties.

Mix, drop on greased cookie sheet (greased with olive oil), and bake 15 minutes at 375 degrees. Store in the refrigerator.

Menu

1/4 cup cooked brown rice,
1/3 cup RAW hamburger, chicken, turkey
2 tbsp grated or chopped RAW vegetables
1/3 cup creamed cottage cheese and lots of garlic
1 raw egg yolk

Mix ingredients together and serve.

You can give some dry pet food if it is without preservatives BHT, BHA, or Ethyoxoquin.

ENZYMES are only in RAW food. WE NEED ENZYMES TO STAY WELL. See "Pottenger's Cats", page 67.

"Raw Meaty Bones Promote Health" by Dr. Tom Lonsdale, page 68.

Wheat Grass

I took a large round, low clay pot, filled it with good soil, scatterered wheat seeds in it, and kept it moist. The cats love to eat the fresh grass, especially indoor kitties. I dilute 1/2 teaspoon of Pau D'Arco extract with 1 cup of good water to water and use it to water the plants. This really makes the plants grow.

Helpful Hints

My animals get daily chlorophyll in water, plenty of garlic, some raw meat, and egg yolk. When I notice a system weakening I add certain herbs. For example for eye problems, I would add Eyebright Plus and Pau D'Arco. Six drops of undiluted chlorophyll in their food daily makes them healthy.

Write me if you see wild animals barbecuing!

Loss of appetite is usually due to sickness. I'll give them cooked, cut up, chicken livers with raw egg yolk and herbs.

Koko The Gorilla

Koko has a pet kitten and she does sign language. She was on the cover of National Geographic twice.

Dr. Patterson of the Gorilla Foundation, who cares for Koko, liked my book. I sent free herbs for depression (Mood Elevator and Nutri-Calm) as she was being moved to a new preserve in Hawaii.

Small Animal Sleeping Bag

Our dear pet rat, Rachel, enjoys being snug when she snoozes. I save holey socks [cotton would be best] for her and give her a clean one each time I clean her cage. She loves to borrow down into it and use it as a sleeping bag! I'm sure other small pets such as mice, hamsters, and gerbils would appreciate this tip as well.
- from Dorothy Murray, Ohio

RESCUE REMEDY

I've used Rescue Remedy for many problems with my pets. I give it to them several days before and during traveling, going to the groomer's, and when trimming nails at home. If the nail bleeds, I put goldenseal on it and the bleeding stops. To calm a frightened stray, I give it Rescue Remedy. It makes it easier on both of us.

NATURE'S SUNSHINE HAS HOMEOPATHIC DISTRESS REMEDY NOW.

Ruth gave her cat some Rescue Remedy during labor. It helps to calm the mother and they can labor easier. She spayed her after she had the kittens. After surgery it also relaxes pets.

Joe gave Rescue Remedy to his dog after it was in an accident. It helped the dog to remain calm until he reached a vet.

The Rescue Remedy cream is great. I've used it on many occasions. It is easy to apply. Lisa used Rescue Remedy on her horse to get him in the trailer. It used to take her a long time to get him in when he was excited or frightened.

NATURE'S SUNSHINE'S ESSENTIAL OILS

Several drops can be put in a small spray bottle with water to mist around pet areas (cover eyes). LAVENDAR relaxes everyone: traveling, emergencies, and helping the animals to relax to help healing.

Everyone thinks their dog is the cutest, the smartest, and the most lovable dog in the world - and everyone is right!

- Richard C. Miller

Lovey, My 22 Year-Old, Healthy Cat

I've received thousands of calls over the years from people from people ordering my book on herbs for theie pets. Their pets are run down, have one or more diseases, and their vet bills are high; some are $3000.

My 22-year-old Lovey is so healthy; no cataracts, no arthritis, no tumors; and she has beautiful clear eyes and a beautiful silky coat. She's been to the vet for a rabies hot. She never gets any other immunization. Her immune system is very strong.

In the morning she gets some raw chicken, turkey, or beef with minced fresh garlic, raw organic egg, Pau D'Arco or VS-C extract, and any other herb she needs. In the afternoon she gets a quality kibble, such as Pet Guard. Her water, like mine, is reverse osmosis filtered, with some Chlorophyll in it. I keep us sprayed with levender essential oil diluted with water. My Sammy lived to 23 and Katsy to 21 years.

My deepest thanks to vets like Dr. Tom Lonsdale and his book "Raw Meaty Bones Promote Health". I intend to add raw meaty bones to Lovey's diet also. It will improve her teeth and gums also. God bless you Dr. Tom Lonsdale from Australia and Dr. Pottenger of "Pottenger's Cats". See the Books and Articles Section for more information.

HELP SAVE US

Facts about overpopulation:

Two uncontrolled breeding cats, plus all their kittens and kitten's kittens, if none were neutered or spayed will add up to:

2 litters per year.

Average of 2.8 surviving from each litter.

10 year breeding life.

In ten years will multiply to 80,399,780 cats!

As many 10,000 cats and dogs are born in the United States every hour, an estimated 10-15 million dogs are homeless strays; shelters are called upon to find new homes for 7 million cats and kittens annually, but only 4% are placed.

Be a responsible pet owner; spay or neuter your pet!

Contact local animal shelters for information on inexpensive neutering, spaying, and shot clinics.

Many newspapers and radio and TV stations advertise lost and found pets free. Photos are helpful.

No need to search the far corners
of the Earth to find true love.
Search your local dog pound.
                    - Norb Otto

Handy household hint

Save the water from cooked vegetables to add extra flavor and vitamins to your pet's dry food. Allow the water to cool down before adding it to the food.
— Cassandra Kent, author of "Household Hints & Tips" from DK Publishing.

THE FLOOD

GOD SAID: *"It is going to rain.*
    Noah, get busy and build an Ark.
    Don't worry about a place to park.
    Build it big and build it strong.
    I'll send the animals along,
    They'll come in pairs, yes, two by two.
    Will make of the Ark a perfect zoo."

NOAH SAID: *"Whatever You say, Lord, I'm willing to do.*
    Be it build an Ark or take care of a zoo.
    But one thing I don't understand
    Is how such a boat is going to float
    When all around here is only dry land?"

GOD SAID: *"I'll take care of that.*
    Just build the Ark. Forget your fears.
    It will take a hundred and twenty years.
    Then the waters will cover the mountain tops
    And all that's living will be drowned;
    But in the Ark you'll be safe and sound."

NOAH SAID: *"O.K. Lord. I'm on my way.*
    I'll do it just the way you say.
    I'll trust and work from dawn to dark
    Until I've finished all the Ark."

GOD SAID: *"Get going, Noah. Times a wasting.*
    Grab your tools and start creating."

Edna Rutschman, Missionary

Isn't it interesting that Noah could have built a smaller boat for 8 people, but God wanted all the animals saved too! (Wish I could have been aboard.)

TRUE TESTIMONIALS

Allergies, Cancer, Tumors, Arthritis, Etc.

My name is Vicki, and my dog's name is Princess; she is a Terrier-Sheperd mix and weighs 75 pounds. This is a story about my dog.

Five years ago Princess was under a veterinarian's treatment for year-round allergies. The treatment included medicated shampoo, conditioner, allergy pills, ointments, capsules, and shots. None of these helped Princess' condition and she was getting worse day by day. She had started with a small rash on her stomach and legs. In time it covered ninety percent of her body and she was chewing on her skin until it broke open. Her hair was falling out and she suffered from runny nose and eyes, scratching, and vomiting throughout the five years of treatment. Thousands of dollars later, the veterinarian suggested putting Princess on steroids and taking her to a skin specialist. I could not afford to do this. Within the last year Princess developed other problems including large tumors over her body, arthritis, and a torn ligament. She was in so much pain that we talked about putting her to sleep.

When we were about to give up hope, we met Ruth and she told us about experiences she and others have had with pets and herbs. Of course we had our doubts, but we were willing to try anything. Within three days of taking herbs, Princess' skin healed. She stopped chewing on her legs and her hair began to grow back. She is no longer limping and I can tell she is feeling a lot better. Within one week the tumors went away. Her tail won't stop wagging and I can't wait to see what the next month brings as she continues her recovery.

I gave Princess ALJ (allergy combination), Pau D'Arco (blood purifier), Chaparral (general good effect on whole body), Red Clover (terrific tonic for body), Joint Support (arthritis combination), and VS-C (an anti-viral, anti-fungal, and antibiotic combination). Una De Gato could be added now.

Allergies

Kevin is very happy with 'Bart', a beautiful dog he adopted from Stonehead, a dog shelter near Middleburg, Virginia. Kevin takes ALJ and Immune Maintenance for his allergies to dog hair. He also could take our Animal Hair Dander, a homeopathic. Kevin is healthier and able to be around pets now. It's easy to be allergy-free with herbs.

Arthritis

Marge's older dog had athritis and could not walk right. She gave him Joint Support (arthritis combination), CA (calcium combination), APS (pain combination), and a small amount of Pau D'Arco. She could have also used the homeopathic pain remedy.

He walks very well now and looks younger. Herbs improved everything like hair, eyes, vitality, and disposition. It's easier to smile when you feel good.

Arthritis in dog and other problems

We received a blessing in 1985 when I first met Ruth Burton. My dog Misty was a beautiful, smart, beagle mix. She was 5 years old, but had arthritis. Ruth was able to do a lot to control this condition as well as keeping our dog very healthful for the next 11 years. We lost our precious little Misty several months ago at age 16 years but we are forever grateful to Ruth for prolonging her life so we could enjoy her for a long time and thankful for the quality of life she enjoyed. We also have a gorgeous and healthy 8 year old cat who has been taking her herbs since birth.

- Martha

Bad Breath from Constipation

A kitty I found had bad breath. Looking at her eyes I noticed a large dark area around her pupil. I gave her Colon Herbs and her breath cleared up after much dark fecal matter was eliminated. I also gave her VS-C as it is supposed to be good for her immune system. Una De Gato would be great.

Birds

My birds get a fine quality food called 'Toppers'. Cheap foods have too many sunflower seeds in them and fillers. I would rather pay a little more for their food and have them well, strong, and happy. Their colors are unusually bright and beautiful and they are so strong and healthy. The vet was very impressed with their good health. Chlorophyll in water each time you change the water; the color should be <u>light</u> green.

They get a little chlorophyll in pure reverse osmosis water each day. I also spray them daily with a fine spray of reverse osmosis water with a little chlorophyll in it. If I want to add a little Homeopathic Remedy I add it to the spray water. For treats, they like uncooked and unsalted nuts (especially almonds), white unprocessed cheese, and organic fruits and vegetables, farm eggs, and perhaps a good 5 grain cracker, rice cake, or a piece of toasted 5 grain bread.

I put their bird cage out at least once a week for fesh air and protected sunlight. How boring it is to be in the same spot all the time! One bird or pet alone is so lonesome. Most people use cages that are too small.

I find adding a very small amount of herbs to the bird's food or water works great. One bird drinks "DISTRESS REMEDY" from a separate dropper. Keep bottle droppers CLEAN.

Bladder, Anal, and Prostate Cancer in Older Dog

Adno carcinomia of Anal Gland, Carcinoma in bladder, Transitional cell carcinomia, morthologic features are consistant with prostatic epthelium and a Prostatic lesion.

Gail took Spike in October 1995 to a vet and Spike was diagnosed with cancer. It was recommended later that he be put down. Spike's fur and entire look were unhealthy looking. He looked so sad as he must have felt terrible.

Gail gave him Una de Gato, Pau D'Arco, All Cell Detox, Joint Support Concentrate, Keone, Chlorophyll by mouth and in water, KB-C, and VS-C. She also gave him Garlic in his food and some raw turkey as living enzymes are only in living raw food.

The tests came back June 19, 1996 all clear of cancer. We are all very happy but Spike is the happiest.

Gail will keep Spike on a maintenance plan the rest of his life.

Bleeding

Ed's dog had cut his foot and it was bleeding quite a bit. Ed put some Capsicum (red pepper) on the cut and took the dog to the vet. It seems the platelets multiplied and stopped the bleeding in a few minutes.

Ed was careful not to let his dog lick the capsicum; he had a cloth over the foot.

Bowel Troubles

Willie, Carmen's dog, had chronic colitis or chronic bacteria in the G.I. tract or chronic bowel syndrome.

Symptoms appeared at six months through age five years (July 1995). There was diarrhea, loss of appetite, stomach squeals (which could be heard two rooms away), black stools coming from the upper intestine or bright red blood with mucous, or he would vomit blood. When offered food, he'd look depressed and roll up in a ball because he was nauseated and had a tummy ache.

Over the years his owner, Carmen, took him to conventional vets, top specialists, and homeopathic vets, but he did not improve.

Carmen's herbal program is UC3J, slippery elm, Pau D'Arco, PDA (protein digestive aid), All Cell Detox, vitamin B6, and vitamin E. Chlorophyll was added to good water daily.

Today Willie has good, normal daily stools. No bleeding, no diarrhea, no stomach squeals, and no vomiting. He eats two meals a day and is stealing food whenever he can. He is happy. (September 1995). Una De Gato would be added now.

Calming Stress

A vet in Texas was concerned with large steers and cattle being too active with 4H boys and girls. He read in my book about Distress Remedy homeopathic. I also sent a bottle to the Horse Listener, Monty Roberts. The steer calmed right down. Directions on bottle. I double or triple amount if needed.

A vet asks me if I gave my pets Valium to relax them to eat. I said "NO, I give them STR-J Extract, a liitle Lobelia Essence, and some Energ-V to strengthen them". I make a little chicken liver gravy and add a raw egg yolk. Then I add a little to the herbs to make them taste good and add nourishment.

Cancer

Charlene's older dog died of cancer. His son, Stud, had cancer as well. It was in his bones.

Charlene gave Stud All Cell Detox (a strong antioxidant, anti-tumor agent), Pau D'Arco (blood builder), Red Clover (valuable for a wasting disease), and VS-C (anti-fungal, antibiotic, anti-viral). For the bones she used SKL (builds skeleton). She fed him a preservative-free diet with plenty of garlic and Nature's Spring reverse osmosis water with Chlorophyll. She'd use Una De Gato now; Wow!

His fur looks so pretty now and he looks young again. His eyes are bright and he is free of cancer. He loves to play now. We have a new herb, E-Tea from the American Indians, which has been successful for them for many years.

Cat (and Tiger!) Fights

Carol's cat Hoby was in too many fights. She had him neutered and the vet cleaned up a wound and gave him a shot and pills.

Daily now Carol gives him VS-C for infections, Horsetail for hair and skin, and Gentian for weakness and improving blood. He is a handsome gray cat now and very affectionate.

I lived about 8 miles from Carol, and Hoby was staying with me. He escaped and walked home. It took him three months.

I also use Tea Tree Oil. It's a very powerful herb for infections. I also use it for wounds on myself. Historically, it is used for staph, strep, infections, candida, fungus, pneumonia, urinary infections, etc. "Out of Africa", a beautiful wildlife park, used Tea Tree Oil in the wounds of two tigers who had bitten each other.

Cataracts

Rene gave her dog who had cataracts EW (eye combination), VS-C, and a little Pau D'Arco. A solution of EW can be made to bathe the eyes with also.

The dog's cataracts were gone in three months.

She also gave him a proper diet with no preservatives, plenty of garlic, and Nature's Spring reverse osmosis water with chlorophyll in it. The dog looks grand and has much improved overall health.

Constipation with Hemorrhoids

Jo had a kitty with constipation and hemorrhoids. She gave her Slippery Elm and White Oak Bark to soothe her stomach and colon. Good cat food without preservatives helped. She took her off canned food which literally had been dead for months, if not years. She added a little cooked ground turkey with lots of garlic in it. Good Nature's Spring reverse osmosis water with chlorophyll in it was also given daily.

Her kitty smelled better and felt a lot better. The hemorrhoid disappeared.

Cough

Kaye's cat suffered from a chronic cough,. She also shed a lot which required constant vacuuming.

A few months after putting her on ALJ or HERBAL TRACE MINERALS (respiratory herbs), VS-C, GGC (circulation and memory), HSN-W (hair, nails, and skin combination), and Three (minerals and vitamins), her cough was gone, her coat became shiny, and her shedding was greatly reduced. Her general health improved also. She acts much younger than her 12 years. She also enjoys her new diet of ground turkey, veggies, and sprouts.

Depression

Ruth gives her animals Mood Elevator (Chinese herb) for depression. It will really lift them when they are feeling under the weather. Ruth takes it too and they're both happy. Sometimes it's depressing for us when one we love is going though a bad time. Blue Vervain is great for calming and seizures.

Gota Kola is the elephant's favorite food. It's for memory. An elephant never forgets. Ginko/Gota Kola is excellent. It usually grows where there are elephants.

Diabetes

Norma's cat got daily insulin shots for diabetes and her eyes were bad. Norma gave her cat P-14 (pancreas combination), VS-C, EW (eye combination), and a small amount of Goldenseal and Pau

D'Arco.

The cat is now frisky and the veterinarian says she doe[s] insulin shots any more. She said that when the pancreas was built up with the herb combination the pancreas healed and made insulin. The eyes were nourished and healed and her eyesight is now fine.

Distemper

Cherie thought her cat had distemper. She gave her HRPC, VS-C, and Pau D'Arco. By the next day she was playing again.

A daily routine of VS-C, Herbal Trace Minerals, and HSN-W was started.

Diarrhea

Alicia's dog had diarrhea all her life. They tried many vets. Alicia now gives him one Slippery Elm a day.

The diarrhea has stopped and the vet said to continue using it since it works. Her dog is happy and a lot easier to care for.

A Dog Named Hootch (Butt-Wagger to those who loved him)

I first met Hootch when he was living across the street - or rather underneath the front porch of the house across the street. He had been left in charge of a brood of puppies while their mom foraged for food during the daylight. Hootch must have been an older brother from a previous litter and certainly took on his responsibility as such with great seriousness. I would watch from my kitchen window as he scouted out the neighborhood to make sure there were no humans around.. Only then would he let his charges out from under their hiding place. They would scamper out and play in the sun, roll in the grass, chase butterflies, and do all those delightful things that only puppies know how to do. All the while, Hootch stood guard over them all. If someone happened by, Hootch would usher them back to the security of the underneath of that porch. This continued for several weeks, but when the puppies started venturing too near the busy road, I knew we had to do something.

The local dog warden loaned us a humane trap and our work began. Two, or sometimes three, fluffs of fur would saunter over to the cage smelling the tender chunks of fresh meat and the temtation would prove too great. In they'd go and over we went, gathering them time after time until the tenth puppy was caught. I was fairly certain that was the last one, but just to double check, we set it one more time. When we returned, we found Hootch crammed inside. he had been confused and was desperately searching for his charges when, being hungry as the babies, he found those tempting bits of meat. He threw caution to the wind, and so beacme our final catch of the day. We knew what we were going to do with the adoreable babies with the fluffy soft fur and bright brown eyes. Our local humane society would help us to find loving homes for them. But an older, seemingly unfriendly wild dog? We weren't so sure. So we decided to keep him in a kennel in our kitchen, right in the middle of the lives of four humans, two dogs, and three cats. Besides, we had seen the heroic, devoted, loving side to this black and tan dog we named Hootch.

Our newest kitchen fixture continued to keep our lives interesting. I wish I could say this transition from wild to tame was a smooth one, but at best it was just plain interesting . He growled at everyone and everything that walked by his kennel, and in our small house, that proved to be pretty constant growling. He chewed up an antique quilt that happened to be hanging just a bit too close to his new quarters. And he nearly broke his neck trying to escape the leash and collar used for his outings. The rest of the time he's lie perfectly still in the kennel. But it all worked for good. We eventually heard a tap, tap, tapping coming from the kennel instead of the constant growling as we passed by. It turned out be his tail wagging so hard that his butt wagged against the cage. We would be the first humans to be loved by Butt-Wagger.

He came to trust us - actually he came to bond with me in such a special way - a way that I will treasure forever, that he allowed himself to share that trust and love with many others as well.

Hootch never needed a leash. Actually, he never needed anything that had to do with being a dog. He ddn't ftech; he didn't bark (although he did talk!) ; he didn't chase cars or bikes; he didn't fellowship with other dogs. No, he instaed wanted and needed to be with people. As it turned out, his particular fondness was for special needs children.

He first came to school with me during a class pet day. Being a teacher, and an animal lover, I always tried to combine the two. What better a combo than children and Hootch?! So, he came with his unconditional love and his wagging butt. Everything delighted him and he always knew where his love was needed. Since my classrooms are rather diverse, we often have many things going on at once. Hootch would find a child reading a book on the floor to curl up, or a book to lay across if he thought that a child needed a break, or a lap to rest his head on so that child would be calmed, or a cluster of children to lay in the middle of his belly could be rubbed. My preschool disabilities class as well as my resource room students came to know, love, and desire to be with Hootch. The best part of any day was when his butt wagging brought sheer joy and loads of giggles to an otherwise regular school day.

I didn't realize how many lives he had touched until he died. He had became very ill and he was not able to jump up into the truck and go for a ride to school. It broke his heart as well as the hearts of all he touched. Mine especially. The last week of his life I didn't hear or see that wild butt wagging, until the wee hours of the morning he died. He woke me wearly as he tried to find some comfort. I put my pillow and my quilt on the floor and he rested next to me wagging his butt for the last time. It's a time that I will always remember with the utmost appreciation. I count it as one of God's most special gifts.

The days that followed were so difficult while at the same time, so comforting. I received cards, posters, pictures, and books from those whose lives he touched. People at places I frequented asked where he was and remebered him in some swaet story, but always remembered with a smile about that wagging butt!

I miss him beyond what words can express, but he reanins in my heart, my head, and my soul. That heroic, devoted, loving Hootch taught us all about unconditional love and simple expressions of that love. A simple as wagging a butt.

- Cherie

I recommended Immune herbs like Pau D'Arco extract or VS-C extract, Herbal Trace Minerals, Chlorophyll in water til light green color, minced garlic cloves in some raw meat like ground turkey daily. I also use various herbs for specific areas that need help. Distress remedy or diluted lavendar oil sprayed.

Drooling and Weak

Jenny noticed her cat was drooling and weak. She gave her Pau D'Arco, Herbal Trace Minerals for vitamins, minerals and glands, VS-C for infection, and HS-II.

After a few days she showed improvement and was started on a maintenance amount of herbs in addition to a preservative-free diet and good water with chlorophyll. She looks and feels just grand now.

Ear Mites

Florence's dogs and cats had ear mites. She put a drop or two of garlic oil, with a little Black Walnut, Herbal Pumpkin, and Pau D'Arco added to it, in her ears daily for a week. In two weeks she did it again for another week to catch the new eggs hatching. The mites were gone and the cat was happy. POSSIBLE CANDIDA (YEAST, ADD PAU D'ARCO AND GARLIC TO DIET).

Hazel uses 1 part olive oil to 2 parts hydrogen peroxide to clean ears or diluted Tea Tree Oil. Afterwards use soothing Pau D'Arco Lotion. CBG extract would be great (internally and externally).

Epilepsy

Dear little Charlie the dog was having repeated seizures. Alice was told she could not have another dog in the RV park if Charlie died. Alice was all alone and this would be devastating to her.

Alice changed Charlie's diet to a preservative free dog food, added plenty of garlic, and gave him Nature's Spring reverse osmosis water with chlorophyll in it. She was careful to check all treats for preservatives as well. Most treats are preserved and this adds up.

Alice also gave Charlie CA (calcium combination), which has magnesium in it, TS-11 (thyroid combination), and HVS (hops valarium and skullcap). Historically, Blue Vervain has been used for seizures (or STR-J).

Charlie doesn't have any more seizures and his fur is very white and fluffy just like when he was a puppy. His eyes are bright and Charlie is happy. Alice loves her dear companion Charlie very much and appreciates having him with her.

Eyes

Louise's dog had a cherry red spot in the corner of her eye. She gave him EW (eye combination), a gland combination, VS-C, and a little Pau D'Arco.

Things look great now and her dog's overall health is better.

Feline Leukemia

People are writing about how garlic is reversing disease. For a cat, they used one cap of garlic a day.

Joan's cat had feline leukemia. She gave him Pau D'Arco, I-X (blood builder), Herbal Pumpkin (parasite combination), Black Walnut, and VS-C (anti-viral combination). She also gave him chlorophyll in his water and by mouth.

Her kitty became strong as his blood improved and his immune system grew strong and helped his body fight the diseases.

Joan gave smaller doses to her other cats to keep them well. She also gave them unpreserved food, with lots of garlic added, plus Nature's Spring reverse osmosis water with chlorophyll.

Olga has a small income. She gave herbs to twelve stray cats with feline leukemia and a smaller dose to the other thirty-five to help prevent disease. They are all well.

Fevers

My Edna used to get high fevers. Instead of a prescribed drug, she gets <u>Boneset</u> herb which historically induces sweating, cleans and eliminates toxins, and has been used for Rocky Mountain Fever, typhoid, scarlet fever, and yellow fever.

Fish

Lora put one tablespoon Aloe Vera juice in a ten gallon fish tank - fish thrived. She changed the water in thirty days as it became a little acidy.

Fleas

Sammy the cat needed a new home. I took him in, he's now about twenty years old and the daily herbs and good food keep him alive. He's always had a problem with fleas and I've come to realize creatures with a low health level have more fleas, just as parasites appear when food is left out.

He was so bad one time he was practically bald. Now he gets herbs and lots of garlic daily. He's so handsome with long thick fur and plays a lot. He gets daily: Pau D'Arco, Herbal Trace Minerals, Str-J, Liva, Kidney Activator, and HSV Complex. He lived to 23 years! He's so lovable - but aren't they all?

I'm told a small amount of apple cider vinegar in the drinking water keeps fleas off pets.

A succesful manager in Arizon says she uses lots of garlic and they never have flea problems.

Flies

Cherie's remedy to keep flies off horses and other animals' faces:

Simmer 8 oz. olive oil and 8 oz. chopped garlic cloves about 8 minutes. remove from stove and strain. Add 8 Oz. rubbing alcohol. Put into spray bottle and cover animal's eyes with cloth while spraying. She also dabs it on their ears.

EQUINE RESCUE SAYS IT'S BETTER THAN ANY COMMERCIAL PRODUCT.

Goats - scours and wasting disease

Last year after kidding, our goat, Cupcake, began having diarrhea, known as scours. After several weeks, with no change in her condition, she was eating well and producing milk, but becoming overly thin. I consulted our veterinarian and he believed she had a wasting disease known as Johne's. He said there was nothing he could do for her and that she was not in pain but would continue to waste away and eventually die.

At this point I called Ruth and she recommended a regiment of Slippery Elm, Pau D'Arco, and garlic. I didn't see any change for several weeks, but by the end of summer Cupcake's diarrhea had stopped, and she was beginning to have normally formed berries as goats should. I continued the regiment through September and successfully bred Cupcake in October. An additional benefit of the garlic was that her coat became shiny and full, and she didn't need any deworming medicine.

- Becky

(Cupcake gave birth to three beautiful babies and her milk is so rich and white.) She had four this year.

GME - incurable infection of the central nervous system ???

Max began to shake on April 10, 1992. He was restless and could not seem to get comfortable in any position. At first, I thought it was a minor infection and that he would beat it back within a day or two. When Max began to pace in tight circles, always to his right side, I suspected a larger problem. The local veterinarian diagnosed Max's malady as a slipped disc and required a full set of radiographs. The radiographs did not bear out the diagnosis. Max's condition worsened. Soon he was unable to move on his own power. He experienced convulsions and tremors. The local veterinarian began administering tetracycline and steroids; then, referred Max to a neurological specialist in a nearby town. While at the neurologist's office, Max stopped breathing. The doctors worked frantically to restore Max's respiration and were successful after many tense moments. These doctors began administering a broad-spectrum antibiotic and IV fluids. Max did not respond. The doctors ruled out the structural damage originally suspected by my local veterinarian. Instead, They suggested that I see a set of neuropathologists in a more distant town. Max's condition continued to be criticalAfter two spinal taps, an MRI and various other diagnostic procedures, the neuropathologists diagnosed Max with several bacterial infections of the central nervous system and began to administer specially-targeted IV antibiotics. Max began to respond slowly. After several days, he was able to eat and drink almost normally. He was released to come home and scheduled to finish his antibiotic regime via oral medication. Max seemed almost normal.

Just prior to finishing his last dose of oral medication, Max suffered a relapse. The neuropathologists performed another spinal tap, but could not diagnose the problem. Max went through several cycles of relapse and recovery. Based on the behavior of the disease, the doctors decided that Max had GME, an incurable infection of the central nervous system. They predicted that Max would not survive the year.

After receiving this dismal prognosis, I took Max to another set of specialists. Following a very thorough examination, they too, diagnosed Max with GME and said that he would not live for very long. They began steroid treatment to ease the discomfort. Max and I were disconsolate.

At this time, Max and I met Ruth. She said herbs could help Max. Immediately, we started LDM 100, Bee Pollen, Chlorophyll, and Brewer's Yeast, in addition to the steroids prescribed by the traditional veterinarians. Max showed rapid recovery. After finishing the LDM 100, Max was placed on a mixture of Immune Maintenance, GGC, HVS, Pau D'Arco, CA, Combination #8, and VS-C. These herbs were specifically selected to enhance the nervous system.

Today, June 8, 1993, more than a year after the initial prediction of death, Max is energetic, bright-eyed, and nearly as mobile as a pup. He suffers some residual tremors due to scarred brain tissue, but seems well in nearly every other aspect. He has continued on the herbs. He still takes small quantities of steroids. I am sure Max would not be here today, if not for Ruth and the herbs. Max and I count every day together as a blessing.

-Jeff

I SUGGESTED, WHEN WELL, TO CONTINUE WITH MAINTENANCE AMOUNTS THROUGH LIFETIME.

Hair Loss

Ruth's dog Pupper, was shedding a lot and his coat was very dull. She gave him HSN-W (hair, skin and nails combination), VS-C, and a proper diet.

His coat is beautiful and shiny and sheds very little. It has a lovely gloss to it. His eyes are brighter and he appears much younger. Good health reflects pretty skin, shiny hair, bright eyes, ar
When we are healthy we look good and feel good.

Hair Loss and Hot Spots

Arlene uses 2 oz. Pau D'Arco lotion, 2 oz. Aloe Vera Gel, 1/2 bottle of Tree Tea oil, and 4 dropperfuls of Black Walnut Extract on hot spots. Works great! Herbal Trim Skin Treatment would also help.

HAIR LOSS IS DUE TO HEALTH LOSS.

Heart Trouble (for Heartworm see Valley Fever)

Olga's rooster had heart trouble. It was Olga's favorite pet. She really loved him. She gave him a very small amount of HS-11 (heart combination) daily.

He's well and happy now and very strong. COQ10 would be great.

Hip Displasia

Micah's dog had Hip Displasia He gave him Joint Support (arthritic combination), SKL (skeleton combination), a small amount of Pau D'Arco and Herbal Trace Minerals for glands and vitamins and minerals.

He found out the muscle holding the hip was weak so he gave him a good dose of Nature's Sunshine Vitamin C and Bioflavornoids each day.

The dog was also given a good preservative-free diet with plenty of garlic and Nature's Spring reverse osmosis water with Chlorophyll.

Micah says the dog walks normally now and is in much better health.

Race Horse - Swollen Legs

A friend rescued a race horse from slaughter. His legs were very swollen. She gave him Bon-C to strengthen the bones and IF-C for the swelling. She added Pau D'Arco to improve the blood system.

How wonderful that he got in good health and wasn't thrown away to slaughter.

Spraying with some lavendar essential oil diluted in water helped his discomfort and pain while healing.

Hyperactivity in Dogs

Daily exercise is very important along with proper food with garlic. Keeping the immune system healthy with Pau D'Arco or VS-C is great. Chlorophyll in the water is essential (when not eating and sick give it undiluted by mouth). There are herbs like the homeopathic "Distress Remedy" given daily. I just put a little on the outside of the mouth or where there isn't hair (like the inside of the ear or stomach) several times a day. STR-J is also great. The drugs are very expensive and have to be filtered through the liver and kidneys, etc.

Limping from Foreign Object

Chocolate limped for several days. Anna Mae couldn't find what was in her foot. She gave her PLS combination to draw anything out and also VS-C for infection.

The next day he was walking normally.

Loss of Appetite and No Elimination

Arlo the dog hadn't eaten for a few days and wasn't eliminating normally.

His owner Joe was out of work and didn't have any money but Joe wanted to help the dog he loved. Joe said Arlo looked bony and extremely thin.

Joe gave him some Slippery Elm and VS-C (anti-viral herb combination). This soothed and fed the dog. In a few days he was filling out and playing and eating. Joe and Arlo were both feeling much better.

Lung Problems

Ruth found Tux in a garbage dump. The cat nearly died, as she had problems with her lungs.

Ruth gave her LH (lung combination), VS-C (anti-viral combination), Herbal Pumpkin (parasite combination), and a little Pau D'Arco. She also put a vaporizor with Tei Fu oil near Tux's bed at night to make her breathe easier.

That was eight years ago. Tux is strong and healthy now with long black fur.

Lyme's Disease

Jinx, Janet's dog, for several months would occasionally cry out in pain. A trip to vet for X-rays showed nothing. Jinx had severe body tremors and slept curled up in a tight ball. Lyme's Disease was diagnosed and Jinx was put on antibiotics. She was having trouble with any jumping movements and needed assistance even getting into a car.

Janet gave her Oregon Grape, VS-C, and Blue Vervain, and VS-C.

After taking the herbs she moves freely, jumping off and on high places, and has no tremors. The Blue Vervain has gotten her through several extremely bad electrical storms, which she feared greatly since being a puppy. A vet check yesterday shows Jinx to be in good health and she now sprawls out peacefuly when resting.

Mange

Winston had Demodex, a mange that is fatal for St. Bernards. His owner, Gary, gave him Pau D'Arco, Red Clover, HSN-W, Chlorophyll, and BPX. His hair has grown in and he's healthy.

Herbal Trim Skin Treatment would be used externally (or Pau D'Arco lotion).

Newborn Kitties and Puppies

When Ruth is trying to save motherless ones she uses Tofu Mo or raw milk with some Slippery Elm and a little bee pollen and Herbal Trace Minerals and VS-C. She uses a little nursing bottle or dropper.

You can return little birds to their nest if they fall out. The mother will accept them back.

Different humane organizations give advice on treating baby animals but herbs seem very effective. No pasteurized milk; Tofu or soy milk. Energ V would be great, and Slippery Elm.

Many female animals will adopt babies from other species that have lost their mothers and nurse them as their own.

Nicks and Scratches on Horse or others

Cherie's horse had some scratches and nicks on her coat.

Cherie opened a vitamin E capsule and spread it on the scratches and nicks. She also used Aloe Vera Gel.

The new hair that grew in was even prettier than the old. The scars disappeared.

Overbreeding and Inbreeding

Anna Mae took a cat that had been continuously overbred into her home to give Anatasia a few months of rest and happiness she had never known. Anatasia's one tooth was hanging out, she was skin and bones, and so terribly weak. She had never known care and love.

Anna Mae gave her VS-C to build her immune system, a little Pau D'Arco to build her blood, Herbal Pumpkin and Black Walnut (parasite cleansers), and FC with Dong Quai (female building combination). She also gave her a little HVS (nerve combination) to relax her.

Anatasia is now six years older. She is plump and shiny and bright eyed. Her tooth fell out, but she looks and feels marvelous. However she remembers the abuse she got when she was young and trusts no one but Anna Mae.

CHECK LIVING CONDITIONS IF YOU GO TO A BREEDER. NO ANIMAL SHOULD BE <u>ABUSED</u> BY <u>USING</u> IT AS A <u>FACTORY</u> AND LIVING IN FILTH.

Parvo

Carol's dog had Parvo. She gave him Slippery Elm, Pau D'Arco, Chlorophyll, VS-C (anti-viral combination), and Black Walnut every four hours for several days until she saw that the vomiting and diarrhea had stopped.

She continued with smaller doses until the dog had totally recovered. She continues to give the dog maintenance amounts of herbs along with a good diet and reverse osmosis water with Chlorophyll in it.

Carol Poore is my manager and I attend interesting and informative lectures that she gives each week. In the group we share our success stories. Most of us came into Nature's Sunshine quite ill.

Rattlesnake Bites - Poisons

Peter Bigfoot, who has a wonderful survival school and camp, has a remedy for rattlesnake bites. One person was bitten and he took Grapevine and Black Cohosh while on the way to the hospital. When he got there he was fine. He took the serum also.

I heard of a horse that was bitten by a rattlesnake and they put charcoal in his water.

Charcoal saved a cat who had eaten some poison.

Rescuing Strays

Oh, it's so dark and rainy! Oh, I've been hit by a car! I didn't get out of the way quickly enough! They've come back! They're picking me up, thank God! They thought I was dead but one girl said, "Let's look at her. Maybe she's okay!". I'm bleeding and I can see out of one eye, my head throbs and my mouth is on fire! I hurt all over and I'm so scared. They're taking me to Cherie's house. She rescues all kinds of animals. Her mom, Ruth, is there. How tenderly they treat me. I think they've fallen in love with me. It's serious. They give me Distress Remedy to calm me some.

We rush to the vet to see if there's anything he can do. He says I have a concussion, have lost and eye, have a broken jaw, and a broken palate. Then, he has to put me to sleep to wire my jaw and I worry about my SECRET.

They take me home the next day and make me as comfortable as possible in a little, soft, warm bed. They feed me soft nourishing food and herbs. The herbs give me strength, relax me, and help me to heal. Love is actively caring, you know. I try to get well to protect my SECRET.

People after people answer the ad looking for their lost kitty, but no one recognizes me. Don't people understand we can't use words when we get lost or hurt? We need a collar and an I.D. tag. Ruth takes me home with her to Virginia where she works out of her house. Her book, "Herbs For All Creatures", helps us a lot. I feel loved, safe, and hopeful.

One day, when Ruth comes home, she checks on me as always, and becomes so frightened when she sees blood on my bed! She searches fo rme and finds two newborn kittens. She asks me how in the world did my secret survive? I tried my best for my babies. I had a hard time of it when a total of five babies were born. My wired jaw made it difficult for me to attend to them all. One baby is dying, so Ruth rushes her to the vet's office. When she returns sobbing, I know. Her son, Steve, buried my baby at his home.

Ruth continues to feed us her nouishing food and special herbs to make us healthy and happy. How she loves us! She calss us her Fur Children. She has two regular Children also.

The Loudoun Humane Society here in Leesburg, Virginia helps folks like us. They have a vet examine me and remove the wire from my jaw. My smile is a bit crooked now, but I do smile nonetheless. They help me to find good homes for my children. Can't more folks help animals like these good people do? I will miss my babies, but that's the way it is.

I'm still very scared of being picked up by people. I get frantic. Ruth's always hugging and kissing me. It's been over a year since my accident, and I usually sleep high in a closet or on top of her canopy bed. I come to her in the morning and I kiss her. This makes her so happy.

Ain't love grand?
-
Ma Ma Esther

I PUT CHLOROPHYLL IN THE DRINKING WATER AND I FEED THEM SOME RAW MEAT WITH PLENTY OF GARLIC. I USE HERBAL EXTRACTS WHEN AVAILABLE.

Concentrated Ginkgo Gota Kola, KB-C, Eyebright Plus, Combination 8, Pau D'Arco, Mood Elevator. Blessed Thistle after babies come to produce rich milk and Dong Quai.

Respiratory Distress

One of Anna Mae's cats started sneezing and appeared to have upper respiratory problems.

She gave him combination Four and VS-C in a moist treat. When he wouldn't eat it she gave it to him directly into his mouth with a little raw honey. She added Chlorophyll to his water and changed to preservative-free food. She added garlic daily to the food. She also put some Tei Fu in a steamer near the kitty.

Kitty was just fine in a few days. Anne Mae gave her other nine cats smaller doses to help prevent them from getting sick. Some of us like Anna Mae help homeless and abandoned animals.

Scours

Joan used Black Walnut and Slippery Elm on pigs with scours.

Senior Citizens

Ruth's old cat got a good preservative-free diet with lots of garlic and Nature's Spring reverse osmosis water with Chlorophyll in it.

She also got GGC combination for circulation and endurance, VS-C for the immune system, a little bee pollen, HSN-W for hair, skin, and nails, and Herbal Trace Minerals which Nature's Sunshine originally made for pets. All Cell Detox dissolved any tumors and she was given LIV-A for the liver and Kidney Activator for the kidneys. Energ V would be good.

Dear old Katsy lived quite well until she was 21 years old. Ruth's daughter Cherie had brought her home as a stray kitten.

Senior Citizen With Many Illnesses

When we flew into Sun City, Arizona to be with my owner, Ruth Burton, I had been sick and depressed for years. The pain of arthritis and allergies was so bad. Ruth loved me and was trying to make me comfortable. My hair was yellowish with patches of open sores. The drugs weren't healing me. My innards weren't working right. I was a wreck and my roommate Ruth was too. She found me back east wandering around when I was a puppy and took me in. My sad family, which included a lethargic, sick cat named Katsy, wandered into the valley to stay. Arizona, with its beautiful mountains and sunshine seemed so lovely. The Indians are interesting too.

Ruth started attending classes on natural remedies. She listened to famous herbalists, Indian medicine men, and vets who used natural remedies and food without preservatives. We started taking herbs and natural food and added garlic to it. We had real meat also, as Ruth said she'd never seen animals in the wild Bar-B-Quing or opening cans. My oozing and aching and depression came to an end. My hair turned silvery white and glossy; my eyes were free of cataracts and shining and bright. We smelled so good as we got rid of toxins and constipation. It's tough to give up junk food all at once.

Our neighbor Kinki is a depressed, sick old poodle who wants to tell you that he was in so much pain from arthritis and constipation that he trembled. Kinki got the same diet herbs and garlic that we had. His coat became silky and he was free of pain. A tumor he suffered with dissolved, his constipation left, his arthritis and cataracts were gone, and of course he was not depressed. We're still old animals but we look young and beautiful and happy just like Ruth. Thank God.

Candy was seven and had chronic mange and itching. It's the same story. Then came the herbs and preservative free food and garlic. It's the first light we've seen at the end of the tunnel, her owner said. I'll use the herbs and garlic on my horses, burros, cat, and other dogs daily to prevent illness. The vet never had to worm the horses after using garlic. It's nothing really new - Far Eastern folks have used herbs for centuries, also the Indians around the world, and most Europeans use them to prevent illness.

I just wanted to share my story so Ruth has written a book, "Herbs For All Creatures".

Pawfully Yours,

- Pupper Burton

I PUT CHLOROPHYLL IN THE DRINKING WATER AND I FEED THEM SOME RAW MEAT WITH PLENTY OF GARLIC. I USE HERBAL EXTRACTS WHEN AVAILABLE.

Pupper herbs are: HSN Complex, Herbal Trace Minerals, Mood Elevator, Pau D'Arco, and Eyebright Plus. Kinki's herbs are: Jant-A, Slippery-Elm, Herbal Trace Minerals, Pau D'Arco, All Cell Detox, and Mood Elevator. Candy's herbs are: HSN Complex, Herbal Trace Minerals, Pau D'Arco, Slippery Elm, and Mood Elevator.

Senior Citizen Terribly Thin and Weak

Lorraine's dog looked very very thin and somewhat weak. She was giving him the best food but he didn't gain any weight. Only the stools got larger.
She gave him food enzymes and protein digestive aids. He put on weight very quickly and is looking great. Of course she also uses reverse osmosis water with Chlorophyll and the finest food. All her tender loving care is important to the dog too. Lorraine is a groomer and has helped many, many animals. ENERGY V.

Senior Citizen with Stroke, Tumors, and Arthritis

Virginia's dog Penny is 13 years old. She became ill and was diagnosed as having a mild stroke. Virginia was told to let her rest after the cortisone shots and, if there was no improvement, to consider putting her to sleep.

She was in pain, didn't want to eat, held over to one side and didn't want to lie on the other side. It seemed to hurt her and she couldn't even drink water. Two days later Virginia started her on Butcher's Broom (circulation herb), VS-C, and a small amount of Pau D'Arco to build blood. She also put a little garlic oil in Penny's ears to soothe them. A proper diet with plenty of garlic and reverse osmosis water with Chlorophyll was also started.

In about a week, she was eating, drinking water, holding her head up normally, and was perkier than she had been in a long time. At times she even wanted to play. She also had a small growth the size of a small egg on her cheek for the past two years. Virginia noticed one day it was completely gone. Her fur is soft and her eyes are bright. Virginia says she knows that herbs saved her dog's life. Virginia loves Penny and they have been friends for many years. Animals sometimes give us something extra to live for. Energ V and Una De Gato would be great.

Spinal Arthritis

Fancy, a thirty-five year old Palomino pony at the Equine Rescue League in Leesburg, Virgina has spinal arthritis but she is greatly improved. Cheryl gave her Joint Support Concentrate and Pau D'Arco. She can turn her head and neck now and walks free in her stride. Her coat is lighter and brighter in color and shiny.

Strays

A lady called and said she had seen four newborn kittens with one of them dragging a foot for four weeks. Karen picked them up. They were just bones with skin over them. The one kitten had to have its leg amputated as there wasn't one unbroken bone in its leg. The vet said they had been without food or water for a very long time. It's wonderful to report animals suffering, but <u>giving them food and water immediately is necessary</u>. I could not sleep if I watched them slowly starve and suffer. They are so innocent and full of love. Treat them tenderly.

When my pets are sick or I rescue frightened and sick animals I use a diffusor to which I add essential oils like Lavender to the water. It completely relaxes them. The diffuser disperses the oils finely throughout the room or house. I have one oil I use quite a bit. It's called Fir and it makes my house smell like a forest. Herbs can be consumed, rubbed in, or with the diffusor, inhaled. Terrific. Chamomile is great.

Stress

Historically, Blue Vervain is a relaxer and stops seizures, also STR-C and homeopathic Distress Remedy.

Tartar

My cat had some tartar on her teeth. The vet sold me a rubber cleaning tip with ridges on it that fits on my finger (see reference 1). I put a little tuna juice on the toothbrush and gently rub her teeth with it. Also used for other animals. Co-Q10 is also great for tarter problems; also Pycnogenols. May need enzymes and raw food.

Ticks and Fleas and Sprays

Charlene uses a spray mixture of one-half bottle Tea Tree Oil, some Aloe Vera juice, some reverse-osmosis water, and a little Citronella on her pets, yard, rugs, etc.

Tom added about ten drops of Tea Tree Oil to about a cup of warm water and sponged it on his dog and cat. He also added 1 tsp of cider vinegar and chlorophyll to the drinking water.

Herbal Trace Minerals is excellent for glands and against parasites and fleas. Use lots and lots of garlic daily year round. Excellent! Some folks use Black Walnut leaves in bed area for fleas.

Lisa had Lyme's disease and took Oregon Grape and Defense Maintenance. She is fine now. Also add VS-C.

Joe's Dog had tick fever. He gave him four times a day, with VS-C, boneset, and chlorophyl. He recovered nicely.

Ruth washes her pets in Nature's Sunshine herbal shampoo (add several drops of Tea Tree Oil). She uses lots of garlic in her pets' food to discourage parasites such as ticks and fleas.

Harrowsmith magazine says that pesticides "can cause cancer, nerve damage, and mutations in animals and may cause birth defects. There are effective alternatives. I use a citrus-oil spray or a combination of herbs. Health food stores sell herbal flea collars. You can make a citrus-based lotion by blending orange and/or grapefruit peels (don't use the edible part as it makes the fur sticky) then simmering them in water. After the pulp cools, brush into your pet's fur with your hands. I sometimes add brewer's yeast and garlic to my pet's food (or rub those into their fur).

Ticks and fleas are drawn less to healthy animals.
Daily VS-C or Pau D'Arco to build immune system and, of course, garlic.

Lymphatic Sacoma

Joseph John, a large beautiful dog, was diagnosed with hypo thyroid, high probability of lymphatic sacoma. He lives with the Schreibers at "Equissage" where they teach people sports massage for horses in Round Hill, Virginia. People come from around the world to learn. They have a book "The How To Manual of Sports Massage for thr Equine Athlete". They are giving Joseph John Lymphamax, TS-11 with hops, Pau D'Arco, and Eyebright Plus with Lutein. They are adding All Cell Detox for tumors and VS-C for kennel cough.

They say Joseph John looks great now, eyes sparkling, beautiful glossy coat, high spirits, and happy like he used to be; and we hope he gets well. I wish all vets would use herbs daily all their lives. They'd be healthier and live longer.

Dying Abused Horse

My friend Edith Von Stuemer, the president of the Northern Virginia SPCA, rescued a horse near death, who was tied to a tree with no food. The horse was laying on the ground drinking muddy water. The vets had no hope for him. Edith took him to Joy Martin of Comonwealth Dog Training and I sent free herbs, Pau D'Arco, All Cell Detox, IX, HVP, Lobelia, and Energ V. They gave him plenty of love, good food, and wonderful care.

Several months passed and they called me to tell me the horse gained 500 pounds and they were riding him. We are all very happy, especially the horse.

To Get Stronger

Ruth gives her pets (and herself) 10 mustard seeds daily in their food. The mustard seed is the smallest seed and grows the biggest plant. It is very powerful and is mentioned in the Bible in Matthew 17:20. Hanna Kroeger recommends taking this as she feels it helps to avoid many diseases.
Ruth adds Energ V to their food about once a week. She thinks it has anti-aging qualities and is very strengthening.

Dry food is good but Ruth adds some protein such as tofu, ground turkey, ground nuts, good healthy farm eggs or protein powder (Syner Protein). ALSO SLIPPERY ELM.

Traveling and Calming

I put some Lavender, Mandarin, and Marjoram essential oils on cotton balls, and also make a diluted spray by adding reverse osmosis water. I put this in my pets' kennels before I flew with them cross-country. Everyone at the airport asked if my cats were show cats, and I had to reply that they were strays going to their new home in Virginia. The cats had a very good trip and were very calm on arrival. Delta airlines took good care of us. A month before our cross-country flight, I added bee pollen to the cats' herbs in raw ground turkey four times a day. I do this now twice a day, every day; they are really strong.

Homeopathic Distress Remedy, Mood Elevator, and Blue Vervain are great for relaxing. AND STR-J.

I was careful to time my trip in the spring so my pets would not be subject to extreme heat or cold at any point during the trip.

Ulcerated Leg

A vet had a horse whose ulcerated leg would not heal for a year. He was thinking of putting him down. He made a poultice similiar to one used on a diabetic's ulcerated leg; containing PLS, Pau D'Arco, VS-C, and Aloe Vera gel.

The horse is alive and running as the leg is totally healed. The vet is holistic and also does acupuncture.

Upper Respiratory Infection (HARPER CATS)

Over one hundred and ten cats were rescued from filth, neglect, and starvation in Sterling Park, Virginia in April, 1996 (the Harper case). Most were so badly diseased that they had to be humanely euthanized. Dr. Jones of Ashburn Veterinary Clinic and his assistant Renee have worked hard to nurse, spay, and neuter the cats that survived. Two of these were kittens born just before the rescue to Polly. Polly and the kittens suffered from severe upper respiratory infections. They turned to Ruth for help.

They were given VS-C, Chlorophyll, Pau D'Arco, and Blue Vervain. They responded right away. ALSO COMB 4.

Another cat, Bart, also suffered from neglect which had made him deaf. He received Blue Vervain for his nervousness and general run down health. Also he was misted with water containing a few drops of lavendar which relaxed him.

Immediately call the Humane Shelter when you see neglect or cruelty. Some of us care.

Urinary Problems

Joan's cat had bladder and kidney problems. She used Kidney Activator and chlorophyll. Of course she also built up his immune system. Hydrangea seems to dissolve stones. Muscle test first. Also Burdock.

Valley Fever and Heartworm

Marie's dog was in bad shape due to Valley Fever and Heartworm.

She gave him Herbal Pumpkin and Black Walnut (parasite herbs) and HS-11 (heart combination) for the Heartworm. She gave him a LH (lung combination) and VS-C (anti-viral combination) for the Valley Fever. She also used Pau D'Arco. Also Elecampane Comb. Also COQ10.

When she brought him back for another test, the vet didn't believe it was the same dog. All tests were normal.

Warts, Candida, Depression, Allergies, Bad Skin

Tom's poor dog was covered with warts, had Candida, was depressed, and had allergies and skin trouble. He needed a good food with lots of garlic but without preservatives and Nature's Spring reverse osmosis water with chlorophyll. Also Tea Tree Oil.

Tom gave him Mood Elevator (depression), VS-C (immune system), Black Walnut (parasites in head area), and Herbal Pumpkin (parasites throughout body). He also slowly started to add Pau D'Arco and Black Ointment on the warts. Al-J (allergies). Pau D'Arco ointment or Herbal Trim Skin Treatment on hot spots.
He is clearing up very nicely. His ear canals were closed with Candida. Tom used a little garlic oil and Pau D'Arco in the dog's

ears daily. The vet had cut new ear holes, but they had been closed by Candida too. Homeopathic earache is great as well as very diluted Tea Tree Oil.

Weak Chickens and others

Tom's chickens seemed to be weak in the summer. He now gives them chlorophyll in their water for strength and health. He sometimes adds herbs to their food.
The farm chickens who can run free and peck at the soil are healthier and under less tension. Factory chickens live under constant lighting twenty four hours a day and are not free to roam. They are under a great deal of stress and tension and that affects their eggs. In some cases daily antibiotics are given to keep them alive. Sometimes chickens in the factory systems peck at their hearts and die, so their beaks and claws are cut off to prevent suicide. I have pictures of this. I ONLY BUY EGGS WHERE CHICKENS LIVE ON GROUND AND AREN'T FED DRUGS.

Weak Colt and others

Jean's mare gave birth but her colt was weak since the mare lost her colostrum.
She added Blessed Thistle and Marshmallow herbs to the mare's food. After a few days of nursing the colt became nice and strong again. Jean said the herbs made the mare's milk nourishing and strong.

Worms

Jane called and said she gives her horses a lot of garlic. Her vet says worming was unnecessary when he came to tend to the horses. Garlic has been called 'Russian Penicillin'. ALSO BUILDS IMMUNE SYSTEM.

Nasal Tumors, Cancer, Torn Ligament

Last year Bo, our happy, lovable, playful, muscular, and energetic 70 pound English Springer Spaniel, was diagnosed with cancerous nasal tumors. At the time, he was was four years old. The symptoms began with snorting, sneezing, and occasional nosebleeds in February 1999. After a trip to the vet, he received treatment for inflammation, then seemed to get better. Five months later, the nosebleed was back, only worse. X-rays/cat scan determined that Bo probably had a tumor. While getting a piece of the mass for biopsy, large pieces of the tumor came out (thankfully). The bipsopy came back as cancer. Radiation and chemotherapy were suggested to us as treatment, or we could just treat the symptoms. We were told that the tumor would probably grow back very fast. The whole incident took its toll on Bo, who was noticeably weak and had no appetite. I cried and prayed for some way that I could help him.

My prayers were answered. During a conversation with Ruth.about Bo, I was told that herbs may help reduce the size of the tumor, and that by building up his immune system, hopefully, he would be able to fight the cancer. Immediately, we began giving Bo E-Tea and Astragulus Root (found in Una de Gato), chlorophyll tablets, and garlic. We stopped giving him any food/treats that contained any chemicals. We gave Bo a preservative-free dry food and canned food (enough to mix in the herb capsules). Except for a day or two, Bo never "acted sick". He quickly got back to his old self. We were so happy.

Then, three months later, one day (luckily a day I was off work), after returning from the store, as usual, Bo came to meet me at the car, tail wagging and his ball in his mouth, ready to play. I was shocked; he was bleeding profusely. I immediately rushed him to the vet. He lost a lot of blood, and when we arrived at the vet (about 30 minutes), in the back seat of the car I found what appeared to be a tumor. I showed it to the vet who was surprised that the tumor was so large and was able to come out on its own. I was told to watch him overnight to make sure he would not need a a transfusion. He was pretty much back to normal the next day. We added Capsicum to his herbs to control bleeding, increased chlorophyll tablets to four daily, increased garlic to four teaspoons daily, added raw ground turkey to his food, added Pau D'Arco, All Cell Detox (to dissolve tumors), and Three (overall tonic) to his herbs. Bo was doing fine, but sadly, continued to snort and sneeze. Two days later, I found what appeared to be a blood clot in his food dish! Ever since then, he has been symptom free and doing just fine. I pray for his continued recovery and thank God for answering my prayers with herbs.

In fact, in October, after running for miles (as he has always done) through the fields, Bo pulled a ligament in his right back knee. He was limping so bad, but continued to run and play on three legs, sometimes putting pressure on the injured leg, but not often. After being told that not much short of surgery could correct this problem, and that because of cancer, would be out of the question, we started a regime of herbs to rebuild the tissue. We added Bon-C to lubricate his joints, and later added Glucosamine, and JNT-Concentrate. A few months have passed - he runs and plays on all fours, seldom showing any signs of a limp. We also added Grapine and Citrus Biflavanoids to his herbs.

Over the past few months we have discovered that Bo will eat his herb capsules in low fat cottage cheese, and now have eliminated all canned food from his diet. He eats a small amount of dry food (preservative free) , raw turkey with garlic, broccoli, carrots, and apple (raw and mixed in a chopper), brown rice or barley, and low fat cottage cheese. He drinks spring water.

Nearly a year has passed since the first nosebleed. He is still symptom free. His skin and coat are as healthy looking and feeling as they have ever been (perhaps better). He continues to be a very happy, lovable, energetic, muscular, playful, and fun-loving companion. The vet is amazed at his progress and cannot believe the prognosis was so dim about eight months ago.

B.J Harmody
Woodville,, Virginia

Lily, who was dying

When I adopted Lily from the animal shelter, she was so sick as to be near death (the vet told me it was a matter of one or two more days). She was dirty, dehydrated, and depressed. She had been bitten on the throat and ribcage, had infected, gunky eyes, and, at 28 pounds, had every bone in her body showing. She was so weak she was unable to take more than a few steps and had to be carried outside to relieve herself. And, of course, she was blind. This was early July. By mid-September, when Ruth first saw her, she was up to 44 pounds, her wounds were healing, and her eye infection had been cured. Still, she needed a great deal more "building up" - she was still a little weak and thin.

Ruth started her on Pau D'Arco, Eyebright, Target P-14, and liquid chlorophyll, and she began energizing immediately. Within a few days she was running and playing with our other dogs and full of life. Her old haircoat dropped out, and lovely, thick, shiny collie-fur grew in its place (she's a collie and "who-knows-what" mix—we think some kind of hound). We know that she is a senior-aged dog, but the years seem to have been turned back as she progressed in her recovery.

Although her diabetes and cataracts were too far progressed to enable us to reverse the damage, I am convinced that the wonderful herbs Ruth recommended did a lot to halt the progression of her disease, and I could see the very obvious improvement in the general condition and energy level, She may still be blink, but her eyes are bright and sparkling, and she runs, plays, and has a grand time! Her weight is now up to 56 pounds, and the vet is extremely pleased with her progress. She's a far cry from that poor bag of bones last summer.

Her throat wound is completely healed now, with the fur completely grown back over, and she's gained so much weight that we had to let her collar out another notch-but basically, she looks about the same. She's been at several shelter presentations and really enjoys the attention-there's usually not a dry eye in the house after her story is told.

Love, Anne and Lily

P.S. The other dogs, and the kitty especially, really enjoy the chlorophyll in their water every morning-and I like it too!

Volunteers and their pets are appreciated at nursing homes.

INSTEAD OF PREMARIN I NOURISH MY FEMALE SYSTEM WITH HERBS. PREMARIN INVOLVES A CRUEL PROCESS FOR MARES AND COLTS.

Garlic (Allium sativum)

Garlic is nature's antibiotic. The properties of garlic have the ability of stimulating cell growth and activity. It has a rejuvenative effect on all body functions. It is a health building and disease preventive herb and dissolves cholesterol in the bloodstream. Garlic stimulates the lymphatic system to throw off waste materials. Garlic opens up the blood vessels and reduces blood pressure in hypertensive patients. It contains antibiotics that are effective against bacteria which may be resistant to other antibiotics. It is called Russian penicillin. Garlic does not destroy the body's normal flora. This herb contains vitamins A and C. It also contains selenium, which is closely related to vitamin E in biological activity. It contains sulphur, calcium, manganese, copper, and a lot of vitamin B1. Garlic also contains some iron and it is high in potassium and zinc.

Anemia
Arthritis
Allergies
ASTHMA
CANCER IMMUNITY
Catarrh
Cold congestion
Diabetes
DIGESTIVE DISORDERS
EAR INFECTIONS
Emphysema
Fevers
Germ Killer
Heart Disease
HIGH BLOOD PRESSURE
Hypertension

Hypoglycemia
Infections
INFECTIOUS DISEASE
INTESTINAL WORMS
Insomnia
Memory
Mucus
Parasites
Regulator of glands
Skin problems
Toothache
Toxic metal poisoning
Warts
Worms
Yeast infection

Feed Garlic for Health

Garlic should be an essential part of <u>ALL</u> diets for many reasons: it's **SULFUROUS** and helps keep flies, ticks, and gnats from bothering you; it's an **ANTIBIOTIC** and works without destroying beneficial bacteria in the gut; it's **ANTIVIRAL**, stimulating white cell production, strengthening the immune system, helping to fight infection; and it's an **EXPECTORANT** promoting expulsion of mucus from the respiratory tract.

ALONE AGAIN

*I wish someone would tell me what it is
That I've done wrong.
Why I have to stay chained up and
Left alone for so long.
They seemed so glad to have me when
I came here as a pup.
There were so many things we'd do
While I was growing up.
They couldn't wait to train me as a
Companion and friend.
And told me how they'd feed me and
Brush me every day.
They'd play with me and walk me
If I could only stay.
But now the family "Hasn't Time"
They often say I shed.
They do not want me in the house*

*Not even to be fed.
The children never walk me,
They always say, "NOT NOW!"
I wish that I could please them.
Won't someone tell me how?
All I had, you see, was LOVE
I wish they would explain
Why they said they wanted me,
Then left me on a chain?*

At one SPCA meeting I worked at they rescued a chained starving dog. The collar had to be cut out of his neck. It was a puppy collar on a full grown dog and evidently had not been replaced as the dog grew. I check my pets' collars and ID tags often. Harnesses are more comfortable and safer.

KINSHIP OF LOVE

We came especially today
To share a thought or two;
So here we give you our side
And the rest is up to you.

Herbs are not just for humans
They are for animals, too.
We all want to be healthy
And we want good health for you.

Give us love, care, and companionship,
And we will give it back.
Don't you think we want our worlds
To stay on the same great track?

They say that we are "man's best friends",
But you are our friends, too;
So give us both the very best,
For nothing less will do.

We all can't simply exist in a world
Where health is very poor.
You, not us, have the right key
To open up that door.

When you use the key to help yourselves
Please, - help us, too.
That would be so wonderful,
For, remember, We Love You!

M. LaVonne Hajek

DOG

A faithful dog will play with you
And laugh with you, or cry...
He'll gladly starve to stay with you
Nor even reason why.

And when you're feeling out of sorts
Somehow, he'll understand
He'll watch you with his shining eyes
And try to lick your hand

His blind, implicit faith in you
Is matched by his great love...
The kind that all of us should have
In the Master, up above

When everything is said and done
I guess this isn't odd
For when you spell "dog" backwards you
Will get the name of God!

- Nick Kenny, Poems to Inspire

I prefer getting a pet from a shelter. Some stores are getting their animals from pet farms where the conditions are dirty and they are kept in a cage for years. Check the source where animals are kept for breeding.

PET AGE CHART

Actual Age	Equivalent Human Age Cats	Equivalent Human Age Dogs
1 month	5 months	8 months
2 months	9 months	14 months
3 months	2 years	18 months
4 months	5 years	2 years
6 months	14 years	5 years
8 months	16 years	9 years
10 months	17 years	12 years
1 year	18 years	16 years
2 years	25 years	24 years
3 years	30 years	30 years
4 years	35 years	36 years
5 years	39 years	40 years
6 years	43 years	42 years
7 years	45 years	49 years
8 years	48 years	56 years
9 years	55 years	63 years
10 years	60 years	65 years
11 years	62 years	71 years
12 years	65 years	75 years
13 years	68 years	80 years
14 years	72 years	84 years
15 years	74 years	87 years
16 years	76 years	89 years
17 years	78 years	90 years
18 years	80 years	91 years
19 years	82 years	92 years
20 years	84 years	94 years
21 years	86 years	96 years (My Katsy)
22 years	88 years	98 years (My Lovey)
23 years	91 years	100 years (My Sammy)

CHLOROPHYLL

Historically:

Builds high red blood count.
Provides iron to organs and improves anemic conditions.
Counteracts toxins.
Cleans and deodorizes bowel tissues.
Helps purify liver and aids hepatitis improvement.
Improves blood sugar problems.
Aids asthma improvement.
Increases healing ability.
Helps eliminate body odors and halitosis.
Cleans tooth and gum structure.
Improves nasal drainage systems and sore throats.
Excellent tooth surgery gargle.
Soothes ulcer tissues and hemorrhoids.
Revitalizes vascular system.
Improves varicose veins.

Animals know grass is good for them but I give mine chlorophyll because it's unsprayed and organic.

IN DRINKING WATER DAILY TIL LIGHT GREEN. BY MOUTH SEVERAL TIMES A DAY WHEN SICK (UNDILUTED).

EXTRACTS

I give my pets herbs every day to prevent illness. When the symptoms leave, continue to rebuild with the herbs. Sometimes it's not easy to give a cat or little dog a capsule. I then make an extract of the herb. Extracts are easier to give to small animals.

RECIPE

1. Empty 50 capsules into a brown glass bottle (like an empty prune bottle)
2. Add 1/2 cup good water.
3. Shake well 20 times up and down and across.
4. Add 12 ounces of vodka.
5. Shake well 20 times up and down and across.
6. Add 1 teaspoon of Glycerine (get at drug store).
7. Shake well 20 times up and down and across.
8. Keep in dark room for 12 days.
9. Shake well 20 times up and down and across each of the 12 days.
10. On the 13th day let it settle.
11. On the 14th day strain the mixture through a coffee filter into a bottle (or bottles). Makes about 12 ozs.

Historically: **CAPSULE AND EXTRACT AMOUNTS**

4 drops of herb extract = 1 capsule

1 drop of concentrated herb extract = 1 capsule

1 capsule or 4 drops or 1 drop concentrated for each 25 pounds of body weight

In an emergency situation I double or triple the amounts and give it more often. Direct or surrogate muscle testing is great.

UNA DE GATO SEEMS TO BE ANSWERING SO MANY NEEDS.

SUGGESTIONS TO HELP

Buy tuna from companies that guarantee they don't use fish caught by methods that harm dolphins.

Snip six-pack rings before discarding; thousands of aquatic birds, fish, and mammals are killed each year by getting caught in the rings.

Don't participate in balloon launches; the ballons are often ingested by animals who can die from the effects.

Use non-toxic pest control methods.

Buy products that are **not** tested on animals, This includes many cosmetics and household products. Buy herbs, we don't test on animals.

Don't buy fur, leather, or other clothing that exploits animals. Don't buy ivory.

Don't buy products such as rain forest woods or beef raised on land cleared from rain forests. Instead look for products such as rubber and nut crunch candies that sustain the rain forest. Be a healthy vegetarian. Don't buy birds imported from rain forest regions or Mexico. Many of these birds are smuggled in suitcases crammed so tight that most of the birds die before arrival. They are also stuffed into interiors of cars and many die from fright or lack of air, food, and water.

Keep a collar or harness on your pet with your name, address, and phone number. Your pet can't talk, so many can't be returned when found. When moving or traveling use one of the little barrels that can be attached to the collar to store a temporary address.

Taking animals to nursing or retirement homes really helps older people. They come alive when they see and touch pets. Pets have brought people out of comas.

Please have your pet tattooed in case it is solen or lost and keep a name tag on the collar or harness. Many pets are being stolen out of yards by people who sell the pets to laboratories.

A Matter of Interest...

Recently published by Citizens for Health: "The 1992 Annual Report of the American Association of Poison Control Centers is out. NO DEATHS from taking vitamins or herbs were reported in the United States in 1992. In the same year, 10 million Americans suffered adverse effects from taking FDA approved drugs."

When You Spot Animal Abuse

In families stricken by child, spouse, or elder abuse, pets are at risk, too, says the Humane Society of the Unitd States. And reported abuse is rising nationwide. If you witness animal abuse or neglect, it may not be wise to confront the abuser. Instead, contact the ASPCA or the Humane Society. Be prepared to supply the time, location, and frequency of the abuse. Agents will investigate. You don't have to leave your name.

Love

A three year old boy fell into the Gorilla Habitat at the Brookfield Zoo in Cicago. BenteJua, an eight year old female gorilla, with her 18 month old daughter on her back, cradled the boy and carried him to the service door where an attendant picked him up. She sheltered him from the other gorillas.

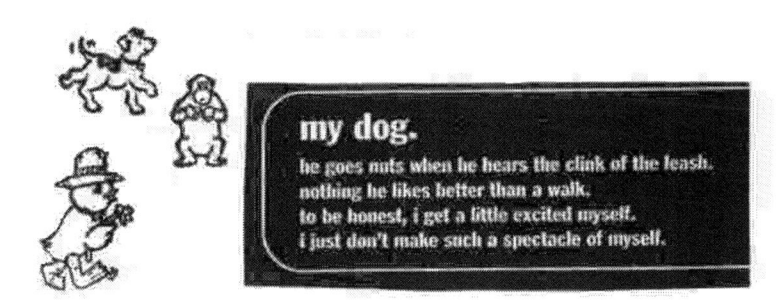

my dog.
he goes nuts when he hears the clink of the leash.
nothing he likes better than a walk.
to be honest, i get a little excited myself.
i just don't make such a spectacle of myself.

ORGANIZATIONS

The Humane Farming Association, 1550 California Street, Suite 6, San Fransisco, CA 94109.
They have a beautiful children's coloring book about humane farming. It's excellent as a gift.

CAARE (Concerned Arizonans for Animal Rights and Ethics), PO Box 33093, Phoeniz, AZ 85067

Internal Fund for Animal Welfare, PO Box 193, Yarmouth Port, MA 02675

PETA, PO Box 42516, Washington, D.C., 20015.
PETA will send a comprehensive listing of companies that do not test products safety by experimenting on animals.

Friends of Animals, Membership Office, PO Box 120016, Stamford, CT 06913-0505

LCA (Last Chance for Animals), 18653 Ventura Boulevard, Suite 356, Tarzana, CA 91356

United Animal Nations, 5892 South Land Park Drive, PO Box 188890, Sacramento, CA 95818-9959.
Rescues rain forest orphans and others.

The Kindness Club, Beaver Defenders, Newfield, NJ 08344
Newsletter, clubs for children.

Dogs For The Deaf, 10175 Wheeler Road, Central Pt., OR 97502

Mission Wolf, Box 211, Silver Cliff, CO 81249
Wolf sanctuary, merchandise, and Adopt-A-Wolf program.

Gorilla Foundation, Box 620-640, Woodside, CA, 94062 (Ko-Ko)

Pamela Brown, Box 5817, Santa Fe, NM 87502 (505) 983-8602

Wolf teacher, travels to lecture
Friends, Inc. (Greyhounds). RD 2. Box 999, Baskine Ridge, NJ, 07921 or 167 Saddle Hill Rd., Hopkinton, MA 01748. Adopt!

Equine Rescue League, P.O. Box 4366, Leesburg, VA 22075

Legislative Tracks, Suite 100, 227 Massuchestts Avenue, NE, Washington, DC 20002
Newsletter that informs about animal realted legislation.

Rikki's Refuge, PO Box 1357, Orange VA 22960
www.rikkisrefuge.com
No kill, all species sanctuary, donations very welcome.

Farm Animal Reform Movement, 10101 Ashburton LAne, Bethesda, MD 20817 (301) 530-1737
This year's World Farm Animals Day campaign may quite literally save 50 billion animals a year by preventing worldwide spread of factory farming.

Pig Sanctuary
Correspondance: RR1,
Box 604,
Shepardstown, WV 25443
Donations: P.O. Box 827204,
Philadelphia, PA 19182-7204
Phone/Fax: 304-262-0080 Email: pigsanct@aol.com

If I can stop one Heart from breaking
I shall not live in vain
If I can ease one Life the Aching
Or cool one Pain

Or help one fainting Robin
Unto his Nest again
I shall not live in Vain

- Emily Dickinson

PET EYE CHART

View at 14'

20/200	♡
20/100	♡ ♡
20/70	♡ ♡
20/50	♡ ♡
20/30	♡ ♡ ♡
20/20	♡ ♡ ♡

1 Bark or Meow	♡
2 Barks or Meows	♡
3 Barks or Meows	♡
4 Barks or Meows	♡

Pet Crisis

Cats and dogs need our help desperately! Each man, woman, and child would have to adopt 50 to 60 cats and dogs a year to give homes to all that are born! To help ease the overpopulation and abondonment crisis, it is important to neuter pets. Innocent animals are dependent upon us for their very lives.

BOOKS AND ARTICLES

<u>Animal Liberation</u> by Peter Singer

<u>The Bug Book</u>, Helen and John Philbrick

<u>The Compassionate Consumer</u>, P.O. Box 27, Jericho, N.Y. 11753. A free catalog that offers alternative products free of animal products and testing.

<u>Health Handbook</u>, Louise Tenney, M.H.

"Herbs for Your Pets", Ruth Burton, <u>Sunshine Horizons</u>, March 1986, page 14.

<u>A Fable for Vegetarian Children, The Story of Thor</u>, If not available at book stores, may be obtained from Namchi United Enterprises, P.O. Box 33852, Station D, Vancouver, B.C. Canada V6J4L6. A delightful coloring book.

<u>50 Simple Things You Can Do To Save The Earth,</u> Earth Works Group

<u>Massage Program for Cats and Dogs</u>, Dr. Michael Fox

<u>Shopping for a Better World</u>

<u>You Can Save the Animals</u>, Michael Fox and Pamelea Weintraub

<u>Your Healthy Pet</u>, Richard Pitcairn, D.V.M.

<u>POTTENGER'S CATS</u> - The Original Study in Animal and Human Nutrition, Francis Pottenger, Jr. MD. RAW FOOD

A comparison of healthy cats on raw foods and those on heated diets. Behavioral characteristics, arthritis, sterility, skeltal deformities ands allergies are some of the problems that were associated with the consumption of cooked foods.

(page 12) <u>RAW MEATY BONES PROMOTE HEALTH</u>, Dr. Tom Lonsdale, Royal Veterinary College, London. Raw diet prevents many diseases and likely there will be benefits of pain-free, happy pets and savings in pet bills.

<u>Pet First Aid</u>, American Red Cross and The Humane Society of the United States.

REFERENCES

1. (page 35) C.E.T. finger toothbrush from VRx Products, Division of St. John Laboratories, Inc. Harbor City, CA 90710

2. (page 36) <u>50 Simple Things You Can Do To Save The Earth</u>, Earth Works Group (also <u>50 Simple Things Kids Can Do</u>)

3. (page 10) <u>Your Pet's Health</u> by Michael Lemmon, D,V.M., Animal Guardian, Vol 8, No 4, 1995 (enclosed sheet).

4. (page 12) <u>Raw Meaty Bones Promote Health</u> by Tom Lonsdale

The Healing Power of Pets

Melissa McKee isn't the only one whose spirits have been lifted by an animal; researchers say our pets truly have the power to heal.

"Pets help people overcome the pain of losing someone close by giving them unconditional love", says Cedar Rapids animal behaviorist Carrie Renshaw, D.V.M. They make us smile, taking our minds off our pain. In fact, nursing homes clients show much lower rates of depression when pets visit regularly.

And that's not all, Dr. Renshaw says: stroking a pet has also been proven to ease stress, lowering blood pressure. "Owning a pet is good for the mind, body, and soul," she confirms.

A PRAYER FOR ANIMALS

Hear our humble prayer, O God, for our friends the animals, especially for animals who are suffering; for any that are hunted or lost or deserted or frightened or hungry; for all that must be put to death. We entreat for them all Thy mercy and pity, and for those who deal with them we ask a heart of compassion and gentle hands and kindly words. Make us, ourselves, to be true friends to animals and so to share the blessings of the merciful.

Albert Schweitzer

THE DONKEY'S CROSS

"Bring me the colt of the donkey" the Master requested. At that, a young donkey was brought to carry Jesus into Jerusalem. The following week Jesus was ordered crucified. The little donkey so loved the Lord that he wanted to help Him carry the cross, but alas, he was pushed away and Jesus was forced to walk, carrying the cross all alone. Sad, the little donkey waited until nearly all the onlookers left. He wanted to say goodbye. As he turned to leave, a special miracle happened, for at that very moment a shadow from the Cross fell upon the donkey's back and shoulders. To this day it remains- a tribute to the loyalty and love of the humblest of God's creatures.

THE HORSE'S PRAYER

To Thee, my master, I offer my prayer. Feed me, water, and care for me, and when the day's work is done, provide me with shelter, a clean dry bed, and a stall wide enough for me to lie down in comfort.

Always be kind to me. Talk to me. Your voice often means as much to me as the reins. Pet me sometimes, that I may serve you the more gladly and learn to love you. Do not jerk the reins, and do not whip me when going uphill. Never strike, beat, or kick me when I do not understand what you want, but give me a chance to understand you.

Watch me, and if I fail to do your bidding, see if something is not wrong with my harness or feet.

Do not check me so that I cannot have the free use of my head. If you insist that I wear blinders, so that I cannot see behind me as it was intended I should, I pray you be careful that the blinders stand well out from my eyes.

Do not overload me, or hitch me where water will drip on me. Keep me well shod. Examine my teeth when I do not eat; I may have an ulcerated tooth, and that, you know, is very painful. Do not tie my head in an unnatural position, or take away my best defense against flies and mosquitoes by cutting off my tail.

I cannot tell you when I am thirsty, so give me clean water often. I cannot tell you in words when I am sick, so watch me, that by signs you may know my condition. Give me all possible shelter from the hot sun, and put a blanket on me, not when I am working but when I am standing in the cold. Never put a frosty bit in my mouth; first warm it by holding it in your hands.

I try to carry you and your burdens without a murmur, and wait patiently for you long hours of the day or night. Without the power to choose my shoes or path, I sometimes fall on the hard pavements which I have often prayed might not be of wood but of such nature as to give me a safe and sure footing. Remember that I must be ready at any moment to lose my life in your service.

And finally, O My Master, when my useful strength is gone, do not turn me out to starve or freeze, or sell me to some cruel owner, to be slowly tortured and starved to death; but do thou, My Master, take my life in the kindest way, and your God will reward you here and hereafter. You will not consider me irreverent if I ask this in the name of Him who was born in a Stable. AMEN.

Animal Parayer Team

*Prayer offered for owner/caretaker
and pet/charge*
animalprayer@yahoo.com
Pager (703)660-5732

Sponsored by St. James Episcopal Church – Leesburg, VA

Does your church have one? Start one.

Four Feet in Heaven

Your favorite chair is vacant now,
No eager purrs to greet me,
No softly padded paws to run
Ecstatically to meet me.

No coaxing rubs, no plaintive cry
Will say it's time for feeding -
I've put away the bowl
And all the things you won't be needing.

But I will miss you, little friend,
For I could never measure
the happiness you brought to me,
The comfort and the pleasure.

And since God put you here to share
In earthly joy and sorrow,
I'm sure there'll be a place for you
In Heaven's bright tomorrow!

- Alice Chase

**Q: Why didn't the worms on Noah's Ark go in an apple?
A: Because they had to go in pairs.**
– Danalee Delossantos age 12, San Diego, CA

All I remember is lying in a daze by the side of the highway. My paws and muzzle were all taped together with thi shorrible stickky stuff and I couldn't move. My heart was pounding really fast.

Every time a car whizzed by I just wanted somebody to stop and rescue me – but I was scared they might run me over instead. After all, I figured I must have done something really awful to be beaten up, tied, and left to die.

So when I finally heard a car slo wdown and oull over, I started trembling really bad. I didn't know what was coming. Wa I ever relieved when kind and gentle hands reached out and oh-so-delicately placed me on the soft seat. Turned out they were Sheriff's officers – and they rushed me to the vet.

What happened next I don't really know because they gave me an anesthetic – but when I woke up a whole lot of my hair was missing! Thankfully, so was the tape. I may have looked pitiful, but I sure felt a whole lot better.

I had to spend some time at the vet – and then some more kind people took me to an animal shelter to finish getting better. Before too long, a wonderful family came by looking for a dog just like me... and now I'm part of their pack.

Can you believe my luck? I get to sleep on the bed, play with the kids, and hang out with a dog and even some cats (who aren't as bad as you might think).

I'm so happy! And I owe it all to the wonderful people who played a part in my rescue – especially the <u>American Humane Association's Second Chance Fund.</u>

I sure hope you'll support AHA so that other animals who are tortured and abused, like I was, can get a Second Chance, too.

Thank you from the bottom of my heart, Your friend, Trooper

A Little Black Dog

From your friends and fellow members in life-study fellowship, Noroton, Conn.

I wonder if Christ had a little black dog,
All curly and wooly like mine;
With two silky ears and a nose round and wet,
And two tender brown eyes that shine.

I'm sure if He had, that little black dog
Knew right from the start He was God;
That he needed no proof that Christ was devine,
But just worshipped the ground that He trod.

I'm afraid that He hadn't, because I have read
How He prayed in the garden alone;
For all of His friends and disciples had fled--
Even Peter, the one called a stone.

And so I am sure that the little black dog,
With a heart so tender and warm,
Would never have left Him to suffer alone,
But, creeping right under His arm

Would have licked those dear fingers in agony clasped,
And counted all favor but loss;
When they took Him away, would have trotted behind
And followed Him right to the Cross.

The Pet's Bill of Rights

Copy the list and post it in your home to remind yourself and members of your family exactly what your pet needs to be happy and healthy. Or give it to a new pet owner as a loving guideline.

1. We have right to be **full members** of your family. We thrive on social interaction, praise, and love.
2. We have the right to **stimulation**. We need new games, new toys, new experiences, and new smells to be happy.
3. We have the right to **regular exercise**. Without it we could become hyper, sluggish... or fat.
4. We have the right to have **fun**. We enjoy acting like clowns now and then; don't expect us to be predictable all of the time.
5. We have the right to **quality health care**. Please stay good friends with our vet!
6. We have a right to a **good diet**. Like some people, we don't know what's best for us. We depend on you.
7. We have the right **not to be rejected** because of your expectations that we be great show dogs or shwo cats, watchdogs, or babysitters.
8. We have the right to receive **proper training**. Otherwise, our good relationship could be marred by strife – and we could become dangerous to ourselves and others.
9. We have the right to **guidance and correction** based on understanding and compassion, rather than abuse.
10. We have the right to **live with dignity**... and to die with dignity when the time comes.

A Dog's Prayer

by Beth Norman Harris

Treat me kindly, my beloved master, for no heart in all the world is more grateful for kindness than the loving heart of me.

Do not break my spirit with a stick, for though I should lick your hand between blows, your patience and understanding will more quickly teach me the things you would have me do.

Speak to me often, for your voice is the world's sweetest music, as you must know by the fierce wagging of my tail when your footstep falls upon my waiting ear.

When it is cold and wet, please take me inside, for I am now a domesticated animal, no longer used to bitter elements. And I ask no greater glory than the privilege of sitting at your feet beside the hearth. Though had you no home, I would rather follow you through ice and snow than rest upon the softest pillow in the warmest home in all the land, for you are my God and I am your devoted worshiper.

Keep my pan filled with fresh water, for although I should not reproach you were it dry, I can not tell you when I suffer thirst. Feed me clean food, that I may stay well, to romp and play and do your bidding, to walk by your side, and stand ready, willing and able to protect you with my life should your life be in danger.

And beloved master, should the great Master see fit to deprive me of my health or sight, do not turn me away from you. Rather, hold me gently in your arms as skilled hands grant me the merciful boon of eternal rest - and I will leave you knowing with the last breath I drew, my fate was ever safest in your hands.

Dump Junk Foods
(Article on Ruth Burton from Sun City Independent)
by Linda Von Tersch
August 30, 1983

Herbs and natural foods can restore health and increase energy levels for many people, says a Sun City woman who applies a health food diet for herself and her pets.

"If people would forget calories and worry about mutrition they would stay slender," said Ruth Burton, who studies nutrition and herbs. "I'm deeply concerned with the nutrition of this country."

A few years ago Burton was unable to lift herself off the couch. A team of medical experts, she said, prescribed medicine that assisted one sympton, but caused others.

"My whole immune system was down. I had liver problems, rheumatism, arthritis, and hypoglycemia," Burton said.

She substitutes sugar with uncooked raw honey, coffee with herbal beverages, salt and pepper with kelp and bio salts.

She wasn't alone as Puppy, a 14-year-old dog, and Katsy, a 14-year-old cat, were also ill. Puppy had lost his hair and had gray on his muzzle and Katsy's white fur had turned yellow and the cat's energy level was low.

The family's health problems began to improve when Burton began using herbs. She is a sales representative for a natural foods company.

Although Burton does not prescribe herbs, she does stick to a diet of raw foods, steamed vegetables, raw goat's milk, whole wheat flour, organic chicken and turkey, nuts, and uncolored cheese.

She substitutes sugar with uncooked raw honey, coffee with herbal beverages, salt and pepper with kelp and bio salts.

While grocery shopping, Burton reads labels carefully so she doesn't buy products with preservatives, additives, and artificial color.

She also reads labels on pet food and is careful not to give her furry friends food filled with preservatives.

Burton said there are few natural pet foods available on the market, but some can be found at veterinarian offices and groomers.

Premarin is Cruel

Meet Marcus -
rescued from slaughter by UAN!

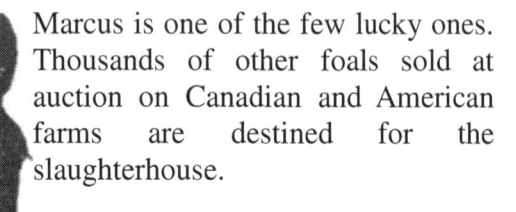

Marcus is one of the few lucky ones. Thousands of other foals sold at auction on Canadian and American farms are destined for the slaughterhouse.

But thanks to a commitment by UAN board member Cara Huff, we bought Marcus at auction with funds from generous UAN donors. Now the young Percheron can live out his life, safe from slaughter, in Cara's care.

UAN works hard to save the lives of horses and many other animals. While rescuing foals from slaughter is important, we must continue to exert pressure for the development and use of non-urine-based hormone replacement therapies.

Please support our efforts by making a generous contribution today.

United Animal Nations
PO Box 188890
Sacamento, CA 95818

(916) 429-2457 Tel
(916) 429-2456 Fax

INFO@UAN.ORG Email
WWW.UAN.ORG Web

My Story... Scooter

I wish you could have seen me as a puppy, but when I was about a year old, I was "dumped" on the side of the road.... and pretty soon after, run over by a driver who kept on going.

Lucky for me I was found by a Pet Adoption Fund volunteer who took me to a vet who said: "His spinal cord has been severed and nothing can be done. Do you think anybody would want him?" Thankfully, Pet Adoption Fund said, "Bring him over."

My new owner got a volunteer who is a carpenter to build my back wheels and boy, do I get around.

Without Pet Adoption Fund I woudl not be alive telling you my story. Where I live, pets picked up by municipal animal control are killed in 5 days if nobody claims them... and who woudl ever have claimed me, after I lost the use of my legs?

Pet Adoption Fund
Devoted to our homeless animals
7507 Deering Avenue Canoga Park, California 91303
(818) 261-6974

ABOUT THE AUTHOR

Ruth is on the November 1994 Nature's Sunshine 'Sunshine Video Club'. It can be ordered from them and is called 'Herbs for Pets'.

Ruth Burton has rescued, sheltered, placed, and adopted countless stray animals over the years. She has worked for many SPCA's around the country and was on the Board of Directors of the zoo in Norfolk, Virginia. She has also been on several radio and television shows to discuss pets.

Ruth handled educational programs for a large shelter in Norfolk, Virginia. She would take domestic and wild animals to schools, hospitals, and detention homes teaching children to leave the wild animals in the woods and show real love to their pets by feeding, brushing, and walking them, as well as getting their pets spayed or neutered.

An interest in herbs started for Ruth when she was very ill over 20 years ago and she feels they were instrumental in her recovery. Her education has included many herb classes as well as couses in Iridology, Reflexology, and Kineseology. Ruth has had the privilege of studying under Dr. Bernard Jensen, Hanna Kroeger, Dr. Neiper from Germany (world cancer specialist), Dr. Christopher, Dr. Parvo Airola, Jim Jenks, Venus Andrecht, Dr. Jack Ritchason, Carol Poore and so many other knowledgeable people.

Putting together her love of animals and knowledge about herbs led naturally to an interest in herbs for pets. Over the years Ruth has collected a large amount of information about how to take care of pets as well as stories from many people about their experiences with pets and herbs. Ruth has now put a selection of this information and stories she has acquired into a booklet, *Herbs For All Creatures*.

Made in the USA
Charleston, SC
24 January 2011